CRITICAL MASS WORKBOOK

IGNITE THE HOLY FIRE OF REVIVAL THAT TRANSFORMS YOU INTO A SUPERNATURAL WARRIOR

MARIO MURILLO

DESTINY IMAGE

Destiny Image P.O. Box 310, Shippensburg, PA 17257-0310

This book and all other Destiny Image's books are available at Christian bookstores and distributors worldwide.

For Worldwide Distribution.

Reach us on the Internet: www.destinyimage.com.

ISBN 13 TP: 9798881500320

ISBN 13 eBook: 9798881500337

CONTENTS

INTRODUCTION

Welcome to the "Critical Mass Official Workbook," a guide designed to take you through a transformative journey of spiritual revival. This workbook is not just about reading; it's about experiencing, practicing, and living out the truths that will be unveiled in each chapter. As we embark on this journey together, you will be invited to delve into profound spiritual principles that have the power to reshape not only your personal faith but also the community around you.

WHAT IS CRITICAL MASS IN SPIRITUAL REVIVAL?

The term "critical mass" originates from nuclear physics and refers to the minimum amount of material needed to sustain a chain reaction. In the context of spiritual revival, it symbolizes the pivotal point where enough momentum is built up within a community or individual's life, leading to a sustainable and explosive transformation. This workbook is structured to guide you to reach and surpass this spiritual critical mass.

KEY TAKEAWAYS FROM THE WORKBOOK

- **Understanding Revival:**

1. Revival is not an occasional uplift in spiritual enthusiasm but a profound and lasting renewal of faith that permeates every aspect of life.
2. The process involves moving from personal repentance and renewal to impacting communities and societies.

- **Stages of Revival:**

1. The workbook details various stages from personal awakening to societal transformation, illustrating how each stage contributes to reaching critical mass.
2. You will learn the significance of each stage and how to navigate them effectively to sustain the momentum of revival.

- **Actionable Steps:**

1. Each chapter provides actionable steps designed to cultivate, equip, and engage you in the practice of revival. These steps are practical and meant to be incorporated into your daily life.
2. By following these steps, you not only grow personally but also contribute to the spiritual awakening of those around you.

- **Deepening Your Faith:**

1. Through reflective questions and journaling prompts, you will explore deeper into your own faith, confront challenges, and celebrate breakthroughs.
2. These tools are intended to help you articulate and solidify your experiences and revelations gained through this workbook.

- **Community and Fellowship:**

1. Revival is not a solo endeavor. This workbook emphasizes the role of community and the power of collective prayer, worship, and service.
2. You will be encouraged to engage with others, share insights, and support one another in the journey of revival.

WHAT YOU CAN EXPECT TO RECEIVE

- **Transformation:**

- Expect to see a transformation in your understanding of what it means to live a revived life. This change will not just be internal; it should manifest in your relationships, your work, and your community involvement.

- **Renewed Mindset:**

- As you progress through the workbook, anticipate a renewal of your mind that aligns more closely with God's desires for you and His plans for your community.

- **Empowerment:**

- Learn to harness the spiritual tools and authorities granted to believers. This empowerment enables you to overcome personal struggles and participate actively in God's work in the world.

- **Sustained Revival:**

- Unlike fleeting moments of spiritual fervor, this workbook aims to provide you with the knowledge and tools to sustain a continual state of revival in your life.

- **Impactful Community Involvement:**

- As your spiritual life is revitalized, expect to become a catalyst for change in your surroundings. Your involvement will bring light and transformation, impacting societal structures and community values.

USING THIS WORKBOOK

- **Daily Engagement:** Dedicate time each day to engage with the material, answer the reflective questions, and perform the actionable steps.
- **Journaling:** Keep a detailed journal of your thoughts, feelings, and revelations as you progress through the workbook. This will be invaluable for tracking your growth and remembering key insights.
- **Community Interaction:** Where possible, discuss your insights and experiences with fellow believers

who are also journeying through this workbook or in your church community.

As you turn each page, let it not just be an act of reading but a step toward deeper spiritual understanding and commitment. The "Critical Mass Official Workbook" is more than a book; it's a launchpad into a lifestyle of revival and transformation.

Let's begin this journey to reach and utilize the critical mass for a lasting revival. Welcome to your finest hour in the pursuit of God's kingdom here on earth.

CHAPTER 1

STAGE ONE: GOD SEEKS A CORE

"Be strong and of good courage; do not be afraid, nor be dismayed, for the Lord your God is with you wherever you go." - Joshua 1:9 (NKJV)

As the author, I want to take you on a journey through the key insights of "God Seeks a Core," a chapter that calls each of us to recognize and embrace the powerful impact we can have through God. It's about seeing our role in something much bigger than ourselves and stepping up to make a difference.

We start with a strong message from 2 Chronicles 7:14, which tells us if we humble ourselves, pray, seek God's face, and turn from our wicked ways, He will respond. He promises to listen, forgive our sins, and heal our land. This isn't just a suggestion; it's a direct call for deep personal and community **transformation.**

Have you ever felt like you're just one person and can't make much difference? Think about people like Mark Zuckerberg or Jack Dorsey, who started small but ended up creating Facebook and Twitter, influencing billions. This shows us that each one of us has the potential to create **significant change**.

Back in the 1980s, Christians began to realize they could claim big things from God—not just personal blessings but real changes in society. This realization should remind us that our faith has the power to **transform** not just our own lives but the entire community.

While people in the secular world chase their dreams with incredible passion, often without the gospel, we have something much greater—God's Word and His Spirit. Yet, sometimes we hold back. Let's pursue our godly missions with even more **zeal** than those in the secular world.

Remember Abraham's discussion with God about Sodom? His negotiation shows how righteous **intercession** can influence God's actions regarding our communities. Our righteousness and prayers can sway God's decisions.

A **"revival core"** is a group of believers set apart to spark spiritual renewal where they live. They don't just pray; they act as catalysts for God's power, making real changes in their communities.

Jesus told us that if even two people agree on something in prayer, it will be done. This shows the incredible power of **unity** and agreement in prayer. What could we achieve if we truly united in our spiritual efforts?

Our leaders are crucial in guiding us toward spiritual **revival**. They need to support and actively promote the full expression of the Holy Spirit in their congregations to help us grow genuinely in our faith and actions.

Knowing who we are in Christ is essential. It's not about feeling good about ourselves; it's about understanding our divine role and **authority** as God's children. This identity gives us the power to face challenges and deeply engage with God's mission.

Revival isn't something that just happens; it's something we choose to engage in. We have a crucial role in bringing about divine intervention on earth, urging us to step up and fulfill our calling.

REFLECTIVE QUESTIONS

1. Think about how you see your role in God's plan. Have you felt like your actions don't matter much? How could realizing your impact change how you act in your community and society?
2. How often do your prayers focus on just your needs versus changes in society? What could shift in your prayers to include more requests for big transformations?
3. Reflect on your journey toward living righteously. How could leading a righteous life make you a more effective advocate for your community's well-being?
4. Consider the leaders in your spiritual community. What characteristics do they show? Do they encourage everyone to embrace and use the Holy Spirit's power?
5. Are you ready to be part of a revival core? What might you need to do to prepare yourself spiritually and mentally for this role?

ACTIONABLE STEPS

- **Cultivate a Prayer Strategy**: Begin building a solid prayer plan that targets not just personal issues but also societal challenges. This might mean setting specific times to pray about things like local government decisions, school issues, or community problems.

- **Equip with Knowledge and Wisdom**: Take time to study the Bible and other resources that discuss leaders like Joseph and Daniel. Understanding their stories can help you grasp how God uses individuals to bring about change.
- **Engage Your Community**: Think about starting or joining a prayer group that focuses on seeking revival where you live. Make sure this group commits to the true purpose of prayer and action, aiming for deep, transformative change rather than just being a social event.

JOURNALING **Prompt**

Reflect on the following: How does identifying as God's chosen influence your actions and decisions? What changes can you make to align more closely with the identity and authority you have in Christ?

CHAPTER 2

STAGE TWO: THE ATTITUDE THAT GAINS ENTRANCE

"Seek the Lord and His strength; seek His face evermore!" - Psalm 105:4 (NKJV)

I want to walk you through "The Attitude That Gains Entrance," exploring what it truly means to prepare ourselves for a deeper connection with God. This chapter isn't just about reading; it's about transforming our approach to spirituality and embracing the responsibilities that come with our divine calling.

We begin with a foundational scripture from 2 Chronicles 7:14, which outlines God's promise to heal and restore us if we humble ourselves, pray, seek His face, and turn from our wicked ways. This scripture sets the stage for understanding the **serious commitment** required to deepen our engagement with God.

You, as the reader, are recognized as someone chosen by God for a special role. This identification is crucial—it underscores your responsibility to live up to this calling by preparing spiritually and morally. It's a call to engage in **intense prayer** that goes beyond everyday requests, aiming instead to reach profound spiritual depths and bring about real transformation.

A key theme is the decision to **set apart for God's use**. This means actively removing any behaviors, relationships, or habits that hinder your relationship with God or weaken your spiritual strength. It's about making deliberate choices that clear the path for more potent spiritual experiences.

The metaphor of standing before a significant door that leads to deeper truths and secrets of God illustrates the tremendous opportunity before you. This door is a gateway to transformative experiences that have changed the lives of many faith heroes. However, as you prepare to knock, remember Jesus' words: "Many are called, but few are chosen." This highlights the **selectivity of God** in responding to those who seek Him, emphasizing that genuine seeking requires the right spiritual posture, not just a desire for revival.

The proper attitude for approaching this spiritual journey is not just about praying and hoping. It involves a sober, serious approach that recognizes your spiritual shortcomings and the seriousness of approaching a holy and awesome God. **True humility** involves seeing the full extent of your need for God and the reality of your spiritual condition, which is necessary for true spiritual renewal and revival.

This chapter also demands a frank acknowledgment of both personal and national sins, drawing parallels with historical and biblical examples of moral and spiritual decline. This call to repentance is about recognizing the real condition of our society and ourselves and being compelled to seek change.

Finally, the chapter underscores that seeking revival is an active, determined effort to do whatever is necessary for spiritual and communal restoration. This **determination to seek revival** means being ready to change your lifestyle and priorities to meet God's expectations. It's about not just participating in religious activities but actively pursuing spiritual depth and societal transformation.

As we delve into these insights, consider how each point relates to your life. Are you truly prepared to approach that great spiritual door? Are your hands clean, and is your heart ready for the truths and responsibilities that lie beyond? Let's move forward together, with the right attitude and a heart aligned with God's will, ready to embrace the profound changes He has planned for us.

REFLECTIVE QUESTIONS

1. How have you prepared yourself for deeper spiritual engagement? Are there areas in your life that need more attention or detachment?
2. How does your current approach to prayer compare to the intense, transformative prayer discussed in the chapter? What steps can you take to deepen your prayer experience?
3. Do you feel ready to stand before God and seek revival? What might be holding you back from being fully prepared?
4. In what ways do you see your community or nation deviating from God's path? How does this affect your approach to spiritual revival?
5. How can you cultivate a more humble and earnest attitude towards seeking God's face, beyond just participating in religious activities?

- **Cultivate a Deeper Prayer Practice**: Develop a daily prayer routine that focuses on depth and transformation, rather than just listing needs. Include time for silence, contemplation, and listening for God's voice.
- **Equip Yourself with Spiritual Discernment**: Study the lives of spiritual giants who have successfully navigated the path to revival. Learn what attitudes, habits, and sacrifices were integral to their spiritual success.
- **Engage in Community and National Restoration**: Actively participate in or initiate community projects that aim to address moral and spiritual decline. Be an example of godly living and encourage others to seek spiritual renewal.

JOURNALING **Prompt**

Reflect on this question: How does the call to prepare for revival challenge your current spiritual practices, and what changes are you inspired to make to align more closely with God's expectations?

CHAPTER 3

STAGE THREE: THE BIRTHING PRAYER

"Call to Me, and I will answer you, and show you great and mighty things, which you do not know." - Jeremiah 33:3 (NKJV)

I want to guide you through "The Birthing Prayer," a chapter that dives into the life-altering experience of intense spiritual prayer. This isn't just about ordinary prayer; it's about those pivotal moments when prayer profoundly changes our lives.

Our story begins dramatically at 3 a.m., when I unexpectedly woke up, overwhelmed by a deep, unexplainable sorrow. This overwhelming feeling compelled me to leave my house and walk the streets in solitude. This episode showcases the **profound awakening** that can come without warning, marking the beginning of a deep, spiritual journey.

During this experience, my emotional and physical states were powerfully affected—I couldn't stop sobbing and was drenched in sweat. These intense physical reactions underscore that deep spiritual experiences can profoundly impact us physically, demonstrating the deep connection between our spiritual and physical states.

Realizing the need for privacy to connect deeply with God, I sought out a secluded place to pray. This **seeking solitude for prayer** is crucial for anyone who needs to engage deeply with God, away from everyday distractions.

Reflecting on the failures and challenges faced in my ministry in Berkeley, I felt a deep sense of despair. Yet, it was these very struggles that pushed me toward a deeper search for God's intervention, showing that our lowest points can lead us to significant spiritual discoveries and a **moment of despair and surrender**.

During this night of intense prayer, I received a divine promise that shifted the trajectory of my ministry, providing a clear example of how **divine encounter and assurance** during prayer can be transformative, affirming our faith and directing our actions.

The next day brought immediate challenges that made me question God's promise. However, unexpected support from a stranger reaffirmed God's message, illustrating that **support and confirmation from others** often arrive precisely when we need them most.

The lasting impact of that night was significant. Nearly 2,000 individuals found their faith through our ministry over the next two years, highlighting the **long-term impact of prayer** on a community and underscoring the power of committed, heartfelt prayer.

Finally, the chapter emphasizes the seriousness and intensity of spiritual warfare during prayer. Like childbirth, this **spiritual warfare and commitment** involves birthing something new and life-giving, often through pain and struggle, but always with profound results.

REFLECTIVE QUESTIONS

1. Have you ever experienced a sudden, intense call to prayer or spiritual action? What triggered it, and how did you respond?
2. Have you ever felt physical effects during or after intense prayer? What does this tell you about the connection between your spiritual and physical states?
3. Do you have a designated place where you can pray and seek God without interruptions? How important is this space to your spiritual life?
4. Can you identify a time when you felt like giving up on a spiritual endeavor? What did you learn from that experience, and how did it affect your faith journey?
5. Have you ever felt that you received a direct assurance or message from God during prayer? How did it impact your decisions and actions afterward?

ACTIONABLE STEPS

- **Cultivate Deep Prayer Practices**: Begin to integrate times of deep, focused prayer into your routine, particularly in moments of personal crisis or when facing important decisions.
- **Equip Yourself for Spiritual Battles**: Study scriptural examples of spiritual warfare and prayer, such as the stories of Hannah and Elijah, to better understand and prepare for your own spiritual encounters.

- **Engage in Community Prayer Initiatives.**
  Participate in or organize community prayer events that focus on pressing local or global issues, fostering a collective effort to seek God's intervention and revival.

Journaling **Prompt**

Reflect on your own experiences with prayer that felt like 'birthing' something new in your spiritual life or ministry. What were the circumstances, and how did you see God moving in response to your prayers?

CHAPTER 4
STAGE FOUR: CRITICAL MASS

"If My people who are called by My name will humble themselves, and pray and seek My face, and turn from their wicked ways, then I will hear from heaven, and will forgive their sin and heal their land." - 2 Chronicles 7:14 (NKJV)

I'm thrilled to take you into the heart of a moment that not only defined early Christianity but also inspired this book: the profound experience in the Upper Room during Pentecost. This chapter, "Critical Mass," explores how a small group of **120 believers** in Jerusalem transformed into a force that changed the world, likening this transformation to reaching a 'critical mass' in spiritual empowerment.

The believers gathered in the Upper Room, holding onto Jesus' promise that they would be endowed with the Holy Spirit and **power.** They were full of questions and uncertainties. What would the Holy Spirit feel like? How would the promised power manifest? Their wait was filled with both hope and anxiety as they contemplated the daunting mission Jesus had left them—to spread the gospel worldwide from their humble beginnings.

Jerusalem at the time was buzzing with the Feast of Pentecost, drawing crowds from across the globe. The city was alive with celebration, much like a major international festival. Yet, inside the Upper Room, the atmosphere was starkly different: solemn, focused, and intense, as the believers devoted themselves to prayer and **waiting on God**. This sharp contrast highlights the often unnoticed yet deep spiritual preparations that precede significant divine movements.

Suddenly, everything changed with the dramatic arrival of the Holy Spirit, described as a mighty roaring sound that overwhelmed the festive noises outside. This divine intervention was so powerful that it shifted the historical spotlight from the Pentecost celebration to this small group of newly **empowered believers**.

As they stepped out into the streets, speaking in tongues, the onlookers were astonished to hear their own languages spoken by those who had never learned them. This miraculous communication led to the conversion of **3,000 people** in a single day, illustrating the concept of 'critical mass'—a point where accumulated spiritual energy results in a large-scale impact.

Reflecting on this pivotal event, the chapter challenges today's Christians to seek a similar depth of empowerment. It critiques modern Christianity's focus on form over substance and calls for a return to the fervor and **power** that characterized the early church. The chapter stresses the need for unity and a collective focus on combating the real enemy—Satan—rather than getting entangled in internal church conflicts.

This narrative isn't just a recount of history; it's a clarion call to action. It invites us to deeply engage with God, seek His face, and prepare ourselves for a revival in our personal lives and communities. By fulfilling the conditions set in 2 Chronicles 7:14—humility, prayer, seeking God's face, and turning from our wicked ways—we can anticipate a contemporary outpouring of God's **power** that can heal and transform our lands.

REFLECTIVE QUESTIONS

1. How does your current spiritual practice prepare you for significant moments of divine empowerment, like those experienced by the believers in the Upper Room?
2. In what ways can you foster a greater sense of expectation and openness to the Holy Spirit's work in your life and community?
3. Reflect on the last major Christian gathering you attended. Did it feel more like the festive streets of Jerusalem or the prayerful Upper Room? What can this tell you about your spiritual focus?
4. How can you contribute to creating a spiritual 'critical mass' in your local church or community?
5. What barriers do you see in your life that might be preventing you from experiencing a deeper move of God?

ACTIONABLE STEPS

- **Cultivate a Prayerful Expectation**: Integrate times of solemn prayer and fasting into your routine, particularly when seeking God's guidance or empowerment for specific tasks or challenges.
- **Equip Yourself with Knowledge of the Holy Spirit**: Dive deeper into the study of the Holy Spirit's role in

the Acts of the Apostles and other biblical texts to better understand and articulate what divine empowerment might look like today.

- **Engage in Corporate Prayer Initiatives**: Actively participate in or initiate prayer meetings that focus not only on personal needs but also on seeking God's **power** to impact your community and the world.

JOURNALING **Prompt**

Reflect on a time when you felt a significant spiritual shift in your life. What were the circumstances leading up to it, and how did it change your approach to faith and ministry?

CHAPTER 5

STAGE FIVE: THE DARK NIGHT OF THE SOUL

"If My people who are called by My name will humble themselves, and pray and seek My face, and turn from their wicked ways, then I will hear from heaven, and will forgive their sin and heal their land." —2 Chronicles 7:14

L et's hold onto the truth that **God is near**, even when He seems far away. The times of spiritual dryness where He feels distant are often the moments He is most actively working in us.

2 Chronicles 7:14

"If My people who are called by My name will humble themselves, and pray and seek My face, and turn from their wicked ways, then I will hear from heaven, and will forgive their sin and heal their land."

In this chapter, I explore a critical stage of spiritual growth and revival often described as the **"dark night of the soul."** This period can feel like a total spiritual blackout, where despite all your efforts in prayer and faith, everything seems to come to a halt.

Imagine working towards something significant, feeling the progress and excitement building, only to suddenly feel like all your efforts are vanishing into thin air. That's what the dark night of the soul feels like. It's akin to **pushing against** an immovable wall.

This experience is similar to a phenomenon observed in **nuclear fission**. Scientists note that right when progress appears to stall, they are often on the brink of a breakthrough. The spiritual parallel here is quite striking. Just when everything feels utterly hopeless, that's often when we're closest to a significant spiritual victory.

This dark night is not just a random tough patch but a profound moment of testing and preparation. It's a phase many spiritual leaders before us have endured at their most challenging times. The real test here is to keep **pushing forward in faith**, even when there seems to be no sign from God.

The purpose of this intense trial, I believe, is to prepare us for what comes next. The praise and challenges that accompany revival can be overwhelming. Without this deep testing, without learning true **perseverance and humility**, we might not handle the next steps well.

So, what should we do when faced with this dark night? We must intensify our spiritual discipline, much like scientists increase the neutron beams to achieve fission. We need to continue **praying and seeking God** with even greater fervor, not relying on our feelings or external signs.

This phase also serves to purify our motives. It strips away any lesser desires and leaves only our deepest longing to see God's glory revealed and to help those who are lost. God watches how we handle this period. If we push through, keeping our **faith and commitment strong**, He sees that we are ready to be trusted with greater things.

In this chapter, 2 Chronicles 7:14 serves as our guiding verse, emphasizing humility, prayer, seeking God, and turning from sin. It reminds us that these steps are crucial not just at the beginning of our spiritual journey but all the way through, especially during the dark night.

Understanding the deep intentions and long-range plans of God, as Moses did, helps us navigate this tough period. It's about more than just enduring; it's about aligning our hearts so deeply with God's heart that we move beyond just witnessing His acts to understanding His ways.

This dark night might feel like the end, but it's actually a gateway to a deeper, more powerful engagement with God. It's about becoming not just a follower who sees miracles but a leader who understands and participates in God's deeper works.

The path through the dark night of the soul is tough, it's confusing, and it can be lonely. But it is also where true spiritual warriors are made. If we endure, if we keep our hearts tuned to God's, the promise of His glory and revival on the other side is immense.

Reflective Questions

1. Have you ever experienced a period in your spiritual life that felt like the 'dark night of the soul'? How did you respond?
2. What practical steps can you take to prepare for and endure through spiritual lows?
3. In what ways can understanding the purpose behind spiritual testing change your perspective on difficult times?
4. How can the church support members who are going through spiritual desolation?

5. What does it mean to you to know God's ways, not just His acts?

Actionable Steps

- **Cultivate Endurance in Prayer**: Commit to regular, intense prayer sessions, especially during times of spiritual dryness, to develop spiritual resilience.
- **Equip with Scriptural Promises**: Memorize and meditate on scriptures that promise victory and presence of God, such as 2 Chronicles 7:14, to reinforce faith during challenging times.
- **Engage in Community Support**: Actively seek support from and participate in your church community, sharing burdens and encouraging one another during periods of spiritual darkness.

Journaling Prompt

Reflect on a time when you felt distant from God or that your prayers were unanswered. How did you persevere through that period? What lessons did you learn about yourself and your faith?

CHAPTER 6

STAGE SIX: THE STEEL PUNCH OF GOD

Hold steadfast in your journey of revival. When it feels like progress halts, remember, this is often the moment right before a breakthrough. Keep pushing with faith.

"Therefore I say to you, whatever things you ask when you pray, believe that you receive them, and you will have them."
—Mark 11:24

The journey to spiritual revival can sometimes feel like pushing against an impenetrable barrier. This is where the concept of the **"Steel Punch"** comes into play, likening our persistent efforts in prayer and faith to a focused, unstoppable force. Much like the **Israeli strategy** against physical obstacles, our spiritual endeavors require relentless, concentrated effort to break through the spiritual resistance we face.

During these moments, it's as if everything stands still; our prayers seem to hit a ceiling, and **God's presence** feels distant. But, it is in these moments, often referred to as the **"dark night of the soul,"** that our true faith is tested. Many have retreated at this stage, but those who persist transform potential defeats into spiritual victories.

As we continue to press on, our **prayers intensify** and we enter a critical phase where our faith either breaks or solidifies into something that can withstand any challenge. It is here that we must intensify our spiritual efforts, undeterred by the apparent lack of visible progress, much like scientists increasing the neutron beam despite the nucleus appearing unresponsive.

This stage of **spiritual warfare** is essential for achieving revival. It's about reaching a **"critical mass"** in our spiritual efforts that leads to a **breakthrough**, often resulting in a profound impact not just on individuals but across communities. It's about creating a **"circle of radioactivity,"** a zone of divine influence where anyone who enters is touched by the power of God's spirit.

REFLECTIVE QUESTIONS:

1. What does the **"Steel Punch"** metaphor mean to you in your spiritual life?
2. Have you experienced a moment of **critical mass** in your faith journey where everything seemed to change?
3. How can you increase the intensity of your **spiritual efforts** during challenging times?
4. In what ways have you felt like your prayers were hitting a ceiling? How did you respond?
5. What does the concept of a **"circle of radioactivity"** in spiritual terms mean for your community or church?

ACTIONABLE STEPS:

Cultivate an attitude of perseverance. When facing spiritual resistance, commit to pushing through with even more prayer and faith.

Equip yourself with knowledge of spiritual warfare tactics to better understand and combat the challenges you face.

Engage with a community of believers to support each other in times of spiritual drought or intense warfare.

JOURNALING PROMPT:

Reflect on a time when you felt close to giving up during a spiritual battle. What kept you going, and what was the outcome? How can this experience inspire you to handle future challenges?

CHAPTER 7

STAGE SEVEN: MAKING REVIVAL PERMANENT

Revival is not just a momentary experience. It is meant to become a permanent change, transforming every aspect of our lives and communities. Keep your faith strong, and don't let the fire die out.

"And let us not grow weary while doing good, for in due season we shall reap if we do not lose heart." —Galatians 6:9

One day, Jesus was faced with a desperate situation. A father brought his demon-possessed son to the disciples, but they couldn't help him. So the father turned to Jesus. When the demon sensed Jesus' presence, it violently threw the boy to the ground, contorting his face and causing him to writhe in pain. **Jesus rebuked the demon** and peace came over the boy, but the boy was still weak and torn. Jesus didn't stop there—He healed the boy completely, making him whole and healthy (see Mark 9:17-27). This story illustrates the crucial move from **Stage Six to Stage Seven** of revival. Satan fears not just revival, but our understanding that **revival can be made permanent.**

In Stage Six, God hears and forgives us. But in **Stage Seven**, He heals our land. There's a difference between God's promise to forgive our sins and His promise to heal our land. **The Steel Punch of God** is felt because God has forgiven us. But now, a void remains, and we must be cautious not to let up. **Euphoria can become the greatest enemy** of revival. People might abuse the excitement, neglect responsibilities, or be led into **counterfeit emotionalism**. Satan might not be able to stop the revival, but he can try to **distort it** by leading us into extremes that discredit the movement.

Revival isn't just a temporary high—it's about evolving into a **pattern of living in permanent revival**. We need to recognize that **revival isn't fragile**; it doesn't just disappear. After the Upper Room experience, the **church demonstrated its power** by functioning daily, not just during moments of intense spiritual experience. The **purpose of this chapter** is to teach us how to make revival permanent. We need to clear away misconceptions from our theology and recognize our **biblical inheritance**. We must understand that Jesus didn't come to **redecorate our jail cells**, but to lead us in a **cosmic prison break**. The purpose that energizes us as believers is entirely foreign to this world.

We've mistakenly tried to make Christianity look more like the modern world, hoping it would be more accepted. But **humanism doesn't work**, and people are sick of it. When they approach the church, they don't want more of the same. They want a **revolutionary call to a new kingdom**. Our uniqueness as Christians has been diluted, and we've lost our **"otherworldness."** The world needs to see a **radical example** of what it means to be a follower of Christ—someone who is truly **transformed by Jesus**.

We need to cast off the lie that we must **add disclaimers** to the gospel. We shouldn't apologize for the hope that lies within us. We must be willing to be seen as different, even if it means risking misunderstanding. The disciples weren't concerned about being misunderstood; they were focused on allowing the **Holy Spirit** to work through them. God saw their willingness and used them to bring **love from heaven** to a hurting world.

We, too, must repent of our cultural mutations of the gospel. We've allowed ourselves to **settle into a passive waiting** for the end times, mingling two worlds that are at enmity with each other. We must realize that **revival** is about capturing the radical, transformative power of God and making it a **permanent reality** in our lives and communities.

The impact of the **Day of Pentecost** on the unsaved was incredible. The Spirit fell with such force that the 120 disciples were **literally thrust into the streets**, preaching in languages they didn't even know. This wasn't just a miraculous sign; it was a demonstration of God's **wonders**. We've lost sight of the **majesty of God**, and our calls for holiness seem unreasonable because they're set against the backdrop of a **puny, distant** God.

On the Day of Pentecost, God was **near, powerful, and awe-inspiring**. The people were both terrified and drawn to Him. The apostles had to know how to channel this fresh devotion into a healthy, growing church. They did this by fostering three key attitudes: **devotion, expectancy, and worship**. These attitudes are the groundwork for **sustaining revival**. We need to cultivate a **devotion** that says, "I'm through with the world and dead religion, and I'm determined to serve God daily." We must maintain a sense of **expectancy**, eagerly anticipating the **gifts of God** and never becoming cynical about the Holy Spirit's work. Finally, our **worship** must be sincere, focused on **pleasing God** and connecting with His heart.

The apostles also instructed the early believers to engage in three continuous acts: **training in Christian character (sanctification), service to others, and prayer**. These acts create a **momentum of blessing. Training** is about **daily repentance** and allowing Christ to be formed in us. **Sanctification** is a life-long pursuit, and if we're not engaged in it, revival is over. **Service** is about touching the whole man with the whole message of the gospel. It's not enough to meet physical needs; we must also address spiritual needs. Finally, **prayer** is the breath of true awakening. It must continue even after revival has started, focusing on keeping the awakening balanced and praying for **discernment** and **protection**.

When these attitudes and acts are in place, God releases His blessings: **visibility, favor, and added souls**. Visibility is about becoming a light in the community, with the **Holy Spirit spreading the word** of our presence. **Favor** opens doors and moves hearts in our favor, allowing us to **influence for good**. And **added souls** are the life of the church—new converts who bring vibrancy and growth. **Making revival permanent** requires us to embrace these principles and live them out daily.

Our goal is to reach **critical mass** and move from the **Steel Punch of God** to a sustained, healthy, and **perpetual revival**. This book may be finished, but the **campaign to bring revival to our land is just beginning**. I invite you to join me in this journey as we follow Christ in what could be the church's finest hour.

REFLECTIVE QUESTIONS:

1. How can we **make revival a permanent part** of our daily lives instead of just a temporary experience?
2. What steps can you take to **avoid the trap of counterfeit emotionalism** during times of spiritual renewal?
3. How does our **cultural mindset** affect our ability to fully embrace and sustain revival?

4. In what ways can we ensure that **our worship remains sincere and focused** on pleasing God?

5. How can we cultivate **devotion, expectancy, and worship** in our personal walk with God and within our church community?

ACTIONABLE STEPS:

Cultivate an attitude of continuous **repentance and sanctification**, allowing God to transform your heart daily.

Equip yourself and others by engaging in **service to your community**, meeting both physical and spiritual needs.

Engage in **persistent prayer**, focusing on sustaining the revival and seeking God's guidance for the journey ahead.

JOURNALING PROMPT:

Reflect on a time when you experienced a **powerful spiritual breakthrough**. How did you feel afterward, and what steps did you take to make that experience a permanent change in your life?

D DESTINY IMAGE

Destiny Image is a prophetic Christian publisher dedicated to empowering believers through Spirit-led messages. Our mission is to equip and inspire individuals to fulfill their God-given destinies by providing transformative resources that resonate with the Charismatic and Pentecostal faith.

We specialize in books, blogs, and back cover copies that reflect prophetic insights, dynamic teachings, and testimonies of faith. Our commitment to fostering spiritual growth and kingdom impact makes Destiny Image a beacon for those seeking to deepen their relationship with God and embrace their calling in the power of the Holy Spirit.

www.ingramcontent.com/pod-product-compliance
Lightning Source LLC
Chambersburg PA
CBHW071511130726
47997CB00006B/2497